POCKET
ASATRU
WISDOM

Edited by: Carrie Overton

"Pocket Asatru" ©2015 Carrie Overton

"Pocket Asatru Wisdom"

©2015 Carrie Overton

Pockect Asatru Wisdom

Volume One ©2015 Carrie Overton

ISBN: 978-1-937571-18-4

Library of Congress Control Number: 2015904649

FORWARD

Pocket Asatru Wisdom Volume 1 is the first in a series of pocket sized books with the goal to provide wisdom and inspiration to seasoned Asatruar and beginners alike.

May you drink in the words our ancestors spoke long before these strange modern days. May the poetry found in these pages remind you of our connection with the earth, with the Gods and with our culture.

It is you and I who will decide the future for our folk. Let us ensure they have something to remember and be proud of.

Carrie Overton

Hail the Aesir!
Hail the Vanir!
Hail the Folk!

VÖLUSPÂ
ᚦᛗ ᛈᚮᛚᛈᚠᛋ ᚳᚱᛟᚳᚺᛗᚲᛋ

1. For silence I pray all sacred children, great and small, sons of Heimdall they will that I Valfather's deeds recount, men's ancient saws, those that I best remember.

2. The Jötuns I remember early born, those who me of old have reared. I nine worlds remember, nine trees, the great central tree, beneath the earth.

3. There was in times of old, where Ymir dwelt, nor sand nor sea, nor gelid waves; earth existed not, nor heaven above, 'twas a chaotic chasm, and grass nowhere.

4. Before Bur's sons raised up heaven's vault, they who the noble mid-earth shaped. The sun shone from the south over the structure's rocks: then was the earth begrown with herbage green.

5. The sun from the south, the moon's companion, her right hand cast about the heavenly horses. The sun knew not where she a dwelling had, the moon knew not what power he possessed, the stars knew not where they had a station.

6. Then went the powers all to their judgment-seats, the all-holy gods, and thereon held council: to night and to the waning moon gave names; morn they named, and mid-day, afternoon and eve, whereby to reckon years.

7. The Æsir met on Ida's plain; they altar-steads and temples high constructed; their strength they proved, all things tried, furnaces established, precious things forged, formed tongs, and fabricated tools;

8. At tables played at home; joyous they were; to them was naught the want of gold, until there came Thurs-maidens three, all powerful, from Jötunheim.

9. Then went all the powers to their judgment-seats, the all-holy gods, and thereon held council, who should of the dwarfs the race create, from the sea-giant's blood and livid bones.

10. Then was Môtsognir created greatest of all the dwarfs, and Durin second; there in man's likeness they created many dwarfs from earth, as Durin said.

11. Nýi and Nidi, Nordri and Sudri, Austri and Vestri, Althiôf, Dvalin Nâr and Nâin, Niping, Dain, Bivör, Bavör, Bömbur, Nori, An and Anar, Ai, Miodvitnir,

12. Veig and Gandâlf, Vindâlf, Thrain, Thekk and Thorin, Thrôr, Vitr, and Litr, Nûr and Nýrâd, Regin and Râdsvid. Now of the dwarfs I have rightly told.

13. Fili, Kili, Fundin, Nali, Hepti, Vili, Hanar, Svior, Billing, Bruni, Bild, Bûri, Frâr, Hornbori, Fræg and Lôni, Aurvang, Iari, Eikinskialdi.

14. Time 'tis of the dwarfs in Dvalin's band, to the sons of men, to Lofar up to reckon, those who came forth from the world's rock, earth's foundation, to Iora's plains.

15. There were Draupnir, and Dôlgthrasir, Hâr, Haugspori, Hlævang, Glôi, Skirvir, Virvir, Skafid, Ai, Alf and Yngvi, Eikinskialdi,

16. Fialar and Frosti, Finn and Ginnar, Heri, Höggstari, Hliôdôlf, Moin: that above shall, while mortals live, the progeny of Lofar, accounted be.

17. Until there came three mighty and benevolent Æsir to the world from their assembly. They found on earth, nearly powerless, Ask and Embla, void of destiny.

18. Spirit they possessed not, sense they had not, blood nor motive powers, nor goodly colour. Spirit gave Odin, sense gave Hoenir, blood gave Lodur, and goodly colour.

19. I know an ash standing Yggdrasil hight, a lofty tree, laved with limpid water: thence come the dews into the dales that fall; ever stands it green over Urd's fountain.

20. Thence come maidens, much knowing, three from the hall, which under that tree stands; Urd hight the one, the second Verdandi,—on a tablet they graved—Skuld the third. Laws they established, life allotted to the sons of men; destinies pronounced.

21. Alone she sat without, when came that ancient dread Æsir's prince; and in his eye she gazed.

22. "Of what wouldst thou ask me? Why temptest thou me? Odin! I know all, where thou thine eye didst sink in the pure well of Mim." Mim drinks mead each morn from Valfather's pledge. Understand ye yet, or what?

23. The chief of hosts gave her rings and necklace, useful discourse, and a divining spirit: wide and far she saw o'er every world.

24. She the Valkyriur saw from afar coming, ready to ride to the god's people: Skuld held a shield, Skögul was second, then Gunn, Hild Göndul, and Geirskögul. Now are enumerated Herian's maidens, the Valkyriur, ready over the earth to ride.

25. She that war remembers, the first on earth, when Gullveig they with lances pierced, and in the high one's hall her burnt, thrice burnt, thrice brought her forth, oft not seldom; yet she still lives.

26. Heidi they called her, whithersoe'r she came, the well-foreseeing Vala: wolves she tamed, magic arts she knew, magic arts practised; ever was she the joy of evil people.

27. Then went the powers all to their judgment-seats, the all-holy gods, and thereon held council, whether the Æsir should avenge the crime, or all the gods receive atonement.

28. Broken was the outer wall of the Æsir's burgh. The Vanir, foreseeing conflict, tramp o'er the plains. Odin cast his spear, and mid the people hurled it: that was the first warfare in the world.

29. Then went the powers all to their judgment-seats, the all-holy gods, and thereon held council: who had all the air with evil mingled? or to the Jötun race Od's maid had given?

30. There alone was Thor with anger swollen. He seldom sits, when of the like he hears. Oaths are not held sacred; nor words, nor swearing, nor binding compacts reciprocally made.

31. She knows that Heimdall's horn is hidden under the heaven-bright holy tree. A river she sees flow, with foamy fall, from Valfather's pledge. Understand ye yet, or what?

32. East sat the crone, in Iârnvidir, and there reared up Fenrir's progeny: of all shall be one especially the moon's devourer, in a troll's semblance.

33. He is sated with the last breath of dying men; the god's seat he with red gore defiles: swart is the sunshine then for summers after; all weather turns to storm. Understand ye yet, or what?

34. There on a height sat, striking a harp, the giantess's watch, the joyous Egdir; by him crowed, in the bird-wood, the bright red cock, which Fialar hight.

35. Crowed o'er the Æsir Gullinkambi, which wakens heroes with the sire of hosts; but another crows beneath the earth, a soot-red cock, in the halls of Hel.

36. I saw of Baldr, the blood-stained god, Odin's son, the hidden fate. There stood grown up, high on the plain, slender and passing fair, the mistletoe.

37. From that shrub was made, as to me it seemed, a deadly, noxious dart. Hödr shot it forth; but Frigg bewailed, in Fensalir, Valhall's calamity. Understand ye yet, or what?

38. Bound she saw lying, under Hveralund, a monstrous form, to Loki like. There sits Sigyn, for her consort's sake, not right glad. Understand ye yet, or what?

39. Then the Vala knew the fatal bonds were twisting, most rigid, bonds from entrails made.

40. From the east a river falls, through venom dales, with mire and clods, Slîd is its name.

41. On the north there stood, on Nida-fells, a hall of gold, for Sindri's race; and another stood in Okôlnir, the Jötuns beer-hall which Brîmir hight.

42. She saw a hall standing, far from the sun, in Nåströnd; its doors are northward turned, venom-drops fall in through its apertures: entwined is that hall with serpents' backs.

43. She there saw wading the sluggish streams bloodthirsty men and perjurers, and him who the ear beguiles of another's wife. There Nidhögg sucks the corpses of the dead; the wolf tears men. Understand ye yet, or what?

44. Further forward I see, much can I say of Ragnarök and the gods' conflict.

45. Brothers shall fight, and slay each other; cousins shall kinship violate. The earth resounds, the giantesses flee; no man will another spare.

46. Hard is it in the world, great whoredom, an axe age, a sword age, shields shall be cloven, a wind age, a wolf age, ere the world sinks.

47. Mim's sons dance, but the central tree takes fire at the resounding Giallar-horn. Loud blows Heimdall, his horn is raised; Odin speaks with Mim's head.

48. Trembles Yggdrasil's ash yet standing; groans that aged tree, and the jötun is loosed. Loud bays Garm before the Gnupa-cave, his bonds he rends asunder; and the wolf runs.

49. Hrym steers from the east, the waters rise, the mundane snake is coiled in jötun-rage. The worm beats the water, and the eagle screams: the pale of beak tears carcases; Naglfar is loosed.

50. That ship fares from the east: come will Muspell's people o'er the sea, and Loki steers. The monster's kin goes all with the wolf; with them the brother is of Byleist on their course.

51. Surt from the south comes with flickering flame; shines from his sword the Valgods' sun. The stony hills are dashed together, the giantesses totter; men tread the path of Hel, and heaven is cloven.

52. How is it with the Æsir? How with the Alfar? All Jötunheim resounds; the Æsir are in council. The dwarfs groan before their stony doors, the sages of the rocky walls. Understand ye yet, or what?

53. Then arises Hlîn's second grief, when Odin goes with the wolf to fight, and the bright slayer of Beli with Surt. Then will Frigg's beloved fall.

54. Then comes the great victor-sire's son, Vidar, to fight with the deadly beast. He with his hands will make his sword pierce to the heart of the giant's son: then avenges he his father.

55. Then comes the mighty son of Hlôdyn: (Odin's son goes with the monster to fight); Midgård's Veor in his rage will slay the worm. Nine feet will go Fiörgyn's son, bowed by the serpent, who feared no foe. All men will their homes forsake.

56. The sun darkens, earth in ocean sinks, fall from heaven the bright stars, fire's breath assails the all-nourishing tree, towering fire plays against heaven itself.

57. She sees arise, a second time, earth from ocean, beauteously green, waterfalls descending; the eagle flying over, which in the fell captures fish.

58. The Æsir meet on Ida's plain, and of the mighty earth-encircler speak, and there to memory call their mighty deeds, and the supreme god's ancient lore.

59. There shall again the wondrous golden tables in the grass be found, which in days of old had possessed the ruler of the gods, and Fiölnir's race.

60. Unsown shall the fields bring forth, all evil be amended; Baldr shall come; Hödr and Baldr, the heavenly gods, Hropt's glorious dwellings shall inhabit. Understand ye yet, or what?

61. Then can Hoenir choose his lot, and the two brothers' sons inhabit the spacious Vindheim. Understand ye yet, or what?

62. She a hall standing than the sun brighter, with gold bedecked, in Gimill: there shall be righteous people dwell, and for evermore happiness enjoy.

64. Then comes the mighty one to the great judgment, the powerful from above, who rules o'er all. He shall dooms pronounce, and strifes allay, holy peace establish, which shall ever be.

65. There comes the dark dragon flying from beneath the glistening serpent, from Nida-fels. On his wings bears Nidhögg, flying o'er the plain, a corpse. Now she will descend.

RUNES

POEMS

TOMS

HAVAMAL

ᚺᚨᚠᚨᛗᚨᛚ

1. All door-ways, before going forward, should be looked to; for difficult it is to know where foes may sit within a dwelling.

2. Givers, hail! A guest is come in: where shall he sit? In much haste is he, who on the ways has to try his luck.

3. Fire is needful to him who is come in, and whose knees are frozen; food and raiment a man requires, wheo'er the fell has travelled.

4. Water to him is needful who for refection comes, a towel and hospitable invitation, a good reception; if he can get it, discourse and answer.

5. Wit is needful to him who travels far: at home all is easy. A laughing-stock is he who nothing knows, and with the instructed sits.

6. Of his understanding no one should be proud, but rather in conduct cautious. When the prudent and taciturn come to a dwelling, harm seldom befalls the cautious; for a firmer friend no man ever gets than great discernment.

7. A wary guest, who to refection comes, keeps a cautious silence, with his ears listens, and with his eyes observes: so explores every prudent man.

8. He is happy, who for himself obtains fame and kind words: less sure is that which a man must have in another's breast.

9. He is happy, who in himself possesses fame and wit while living; for bad counsels have oft been received from another's heart.

10. A better burden no man bears on the road than much good sense; that is thought better than riches in a strange place; such is the recourse of the indigent.

11. A worse provision on the way he cannot carry than too much beer-bibbing; so good is not, as it is said, beer for the sons of men.

12. A worse provision no man can take from table than too much beer-bibbing: for the more he drinks the less control he has of his own mind.

13. Oblivion's heron 'tis called that over drink hovers; he steals the minds of men. With this bird's pinions I was fettered in Gunnlods dwelling.

14. Drunk I was, I was over-drunk, at that cunning Fialar's. It's the best drunkenness, when everyone after it regains his reason.

15. Taciturn and prudent, and in war daring, should a king's children be; joyous and generous everyone should be until his hour of death.

16. A cowardly man thinks he will ever live, if warfare he avoids; but old age will give him no peace, though spears may spare him.

17. A fool gapes when to a house he comes, to himself mutters or is silent; but all at once, if he gets drink, then is the man's mind displayed.

18. He alone knows who wanders wide, and has much experienced, by what disposition each man is ruled, who common sense possesses.

19. Let a man hold the cup, yet of the mead drink moderately, speak sensibly or be silent. As of a fault no man will admonish thee, if thou goest to bed early.

20. A greedy man, if he be not moderate, eats to his mortal sorrow. Oftentimes his belly draws laughter on a silly man, who among the prudent comes.

21. Cattle know when to go home, and then from grazing cease; but a foolish man never knows the measure of his own stomach.

22. A miserable man, and ill-conditioned, sneers at everything: one thing he knows not, which he ought to know, that he is not free from faults.

23. A foolish man is all night awake, pondering over everything; he then grows tired; and when morning comes, all is lament as before.

24. A foolish man thinks all who on him smile to be his friends; he feels it not, although they speak ill of him, when he sits among the clever.

25. A foolish man thinks all who speak him fair to be his friends; but he will find, if into court he comes, that he has few advocates.

26. A foolish man thinks he knows everything if placed in unexpected difficulty; but he knows not what to answer, if to the test he is put.

27. A foolish man, who among people comes, had best be silent; for no one knows that he knows nothing, unless he talks too much. He who previously knew nothing will still know nothing, talk he ever so much.

28. He thinks himself wise, who can ask questions and converse also; conceal his ignorance no one can, because it circulates among men.

29. He utters too many futile words who is never silent; a garrulous tongue, if it be not checked, sings often to its own harm.

30. For a gazing-stock no man shall have another, although he come a stranger to his house. Many a one thinks himself wise, if he is not questioned, and can sit in a dry habit.

31. Clever thinks himself the guest who jeers a guest, if he takes to flight. Knows it not certainly he who prates at meat, whether he babbles among foes.

32. Many men are mutually well-disposed, yet at table will torment each other. That strife will ever be; guest will guest irritate.

33. Early meals a man should often take, unless to a friend's house he goes; else he will sit and mope, will seem half-famished, and can of few things inquire.

34. Long is and indirect the way to a bad friend's, though by the road he dwell; but to a good friend's the paths lie direct, though he lives far away.

35. A guest should depart, not always stay in one place. The guest becomes unwelcome, if he too long stays in another's house.

36. One's own house is best, small though it be; at home is everyone his own master. Though he but two goats possess, and a straw-thatched cot, even that is better than begging.

37. One's own house is best, small though it be, at home is everyone his own master. Bleeding at heart is he, who has to ask for food at every meal-tide.

38. Leaving in the field his arms, let no man go a foot's length forward; for it is hard to know when on the way a man may need his weapon.

39. I have never found a man so wealthy, or so hospitable that he refused a gift; or of his property so abundant that he scorned a repayment.

40. Of the property which he has gained no man should suffer need; for the hated oft is spared what for the dear was destined. Much goes worse than is expected.

41. With arms and vestments friends should each other gladden, those which are in themselves most sightly. Givers and requiters are longest friends, if all goes well.

42. To his friend a man should be a friend, and gifts with gifts requite. Laughter with laughter men should receive, but repay treachery with lies.

43. To his friend a man should be a friend; to him and to his friend; but of his foe no man shall the friend's friend be.

44. Know, if thou hast a friend whom thou fully trustest, and from whom thou woulds't good derive, thou shouldst blend thy mind with his, and gifts exchange, and often go to see him.

45. If thou hast another, whom thou little trustest, yet wouldst good from him derive, thou shouldst speak him fair, but think craftily, and repay treachery with lies.

46. But of him yet further, whom thou little trustest, and thou suspectest his intention; before him thou shouldst laugh, and contrary to thy thoughts speak: requital should the gift resemble.

47. I was once young, I was journeying alone, and lost my way; rich I thought myself, when I met another. Man is the joy of man.

48. Generous and brave men live best, they seldom cherish sorrow; but a base-minded man dreads everything; the niggardly is uneasy even at gifts.

49. My garments in a field I gave away to two wooden men: heroes they seemed to be, when they got cloaks: exposed to insult is a naked man.

50. A tree withers that on a hill-top stands; protects it neither bark nor leaves: such is the man whom no one favours: why should he live long?

51. Hotter than fire love for five days burns between false friends; but is quenched when the sixth day comes, and-friendship is all impaired.

52. Something great is not always to be given, praise is often for a trifle bought. With half a loaf and a tilted vessel I got myself a comrade.

53. Little are the sand-grains, little the wits, little the minds of some men; for all men are not wise alike: men are everywhere by halves.

54. Moderately wise should each one be, but never over-wise: of those men the lives are fairest, who know much well.

55. Moderately wise should each one be, but never over-wise; for a wise man's heart is seldom glad, if he is all-wise who owns it.

56. Moderately wise should each one be, but never over-wise. His destiny let know no man beforehand; his mind will be freest from' care.

57. Brand burns from brand until it is burnt out; fire is from fire quickened. Man to' man becomes known by speech, but a fool by his bashful silence.

58. He should early rise, who another's property or life desires to have. Seldom a sluggish wolf gets prey, or a sleeping man victory.

59. Early should rise he who has few workers, and go his work to see to; greatly is he retarded who sleeps the morn away. Wealth half depends on energy.

60. Of dry planks and roof-shingles a man knows the measure; of the fire-wood that may suffice, both measure and time.

61. Washed and well-fed let a man ride to the Thing, although his garments be not too good; of his shoes and breeches let no one be ashamed, nor of his horse, although he have not a good one.

62. Inquire and impart should every man of sense, who will be accounted sage. Let one only know, a second may not; if three, all the world knows.

63. Gasps and gapes, when to the sea he comes, the eagle over old ocean; so is a man, who among many comes, and has few advocates.

64. His power should every wise man use with discretion; for he will find, when among the bold he comes, that no one alone is bravest.

65. Prudent and reserved every man should be, and wary in trusting friends. Of the words that a man says to another he often pays the penalty.

66. Much too early I came to many places, but too late to others: the beer was drunk, or not yet brewed: the disliked seldom chooses the right moment.

67. Here and there I should have been invited, if I a meal had needed; or two hams had hung, at that true friend's, where of one I had eaten.

68. Fire is best among the sons of men, and the sight of the sun, if his health a man can have, with a life free from vice.

69. No man lacks everything, although his health be bad: one in his sons is happy, one in his kin, one in abundant wealth, one in his good works.

70. It is better to live, even to live miserably; a living man can always get a cow. I saw fire consume the rich man's property, and death stood without his door.

71. The halt can ride on horseback, the one-handed drive cattle; the deaf fight and be useful: to be blind is better than to be burnt no one gets good from a corpse.

72. A son is better, even if born late, after his father's departure. Gravestones seldom stand by the way-side unless raised by a kinsman to a kinsman.

73. Two are adversaries: the tongue is the bane of the head: under every cloak I expect a sword.

74. At night is joyful he who is sure of travelling entertainment. A ship's yards are short. Variable is an autumn night. Many are the weather's changes in five days, but more in a month.

75. He only knows not who knows nothing, that many a one apes another. One man is rich, another poor: let him not be thought blameworthy.

76. Cattle die, kindred die, we ourselves also die; but the fair fame never dies of him who has earned it.

77. Cattle die, kindred die, we ourselves also die; but I know one thing that never dies,—judgment on each one dead.

78. Full storehouses I saw at Dives' sons': now bear they the beggar's staff. Such are riches; as is the twinkling of an eye: of friends they are most fickle.

79. A foolish man, if he acquires wealth or woman's love, pride grows within him, but wisdom never: he goes on more and more arrogant.

80. Then 'tis made manifest, if of runes thou questionest him, those to the high ones known, which the great powers invented, and the great talker painted, that he had best hold silence.

81. At eve the day is to be praised, a woman after she is burnt, a sword after it is proved, a maid after she is married, ice after it has passed away, beer after it is drunk.

82. In the wind one should hew wood, in a breeze row out to sea, in the dark talk with a lass: many are the eyes of day. In a ship voyages are to be made, but a shield is for protection, a sword for striking, but a damsel for a kiss.

83. By the fire one should drink beer, on the ice slide; buy a horse that is lean, a sword that is rusty; feed a horse at home, but a dog at the farm.

84. In a maiden's words no one should place faith, nor in what a woman says; for on a turning wheel have their hearts been formed, and guile in their breasts been laid;

85. In a creaking bow, a burning flame, a yawning wolf, a chattering crow, a grunting swine, a rootless tree, a waxing wave, a boiling kettle,

86. A flying dart, a falling billow, a one night's ice, a coiled serpent, a woman's bed-talk, or a broken sword, a bear's play, or a royal child,

87. A sick calf, a self-willed thrall, a flattering prophetess, a corpse newly slain, a serene sky, a laughing lord, a barking dog, and a harlot's grief;

88. An early sown field let no one trust, nor prematurely in a son: weather rules the field, and wit the son, each of which is doubtful;

89. A brother's murderer, though on the high road met, a half-burnt house, an over-swift horse, (a horse is useless, if a leg be broken), no man is so confiding as to trust any of these.

90. Such is the love of women, who falsehood meditate, as if one drove not rough-shod, on slippery ice, a spirited two-years old and unbroken horse; or as in a raging storm a helmless ship is beaten; or as if the halt were set to catch a reindeer in the thawing fell.

91. Openly I now speak, because I both sexes know: unstable are men's minds towards women; 'tis then we speak most fair when we most falsely think: that deceives even the cautious.

92. Fair shall speak, and money offer, who would obtain a woman's love. Praise the form of a fair damsel; he gets who courts her.

93. At love should no one ever wonder in another: a beauteous countenance oft captivates the wise, which captivates not the foolish.

94. Let no one wonder at another's folly, it is the lot of many. All-powerful desire makes of the sons of men fools even of the wise.

95. The mind only knows what lies near the heart, that alone is conscious of our affections. No disease is worse to a sensible man than not to be content with himself.

96. That I experienced, when in the reeds I sat, awaiting my delight. Body and soul to me was that discreet maiden: nevertheless I possess her not.

97. Billing's lass on her couch I found, sun-bright, sleeping. A prince's joy to me seemed naught, if not with that form to live.

98. "Yet nearer eve must thou, Odin, come, if thou wilt talk the maiden over; all will be disastrous, unless we alone are privy to such misdeed."

99. I returned, thinking to love, at her wise desire. I thought I should obtain her whole heart and love.

100. When next I came the bold warriors were all awake, with lights burning, and bearing torches: thus was the way to pleasure closed.

101. But at the approach of morn, when again I came, the household all was sleeping; the good damsel's dog alone I found tied to the bed.

102. Many a fair maiden, when rightly known, towards men is fickle: that I experienced, when that discreet maiden I strove to seduce: insults of every sort that wily girl heaped upon me; though nothing of that damsel did I gain.

103. At home let a man be cheerful, and towards a guest generous; of wise conduct he should be, of good memory and ready speech; if much knowledge he desires, he must often talk on good.

104. Fimbulfambi he is called who' little has to say: such is the nature of the simple.

105. The old Jotun I sought; now I am come back: little got I there by silence; in many words I spoke to my advantage in Suttung's halls.

106. Gunnlod gave me, on her golden seat, a draught of the precious mead; a bad recompense I afterwards made her, for her whole soul, her fervent love.

107. Rati's mouth I caused to make a space, and to gnaw the rock; over and under me were the Jotun's ways: thus I my head did peril.

108. Of a well-assumed form I made good use: few things fail the wise; for Odhrærir is now come up to men's earthly dwellings.

109. 'Tis to me doubtful that I could have come from the Jotun's courts, had not Gunnlod aided me, that good damsel, over whom I laid my arm.

110. On the day following came the Hrimthursar, to learn something of the High One, in the High One's hall: after Bolverk they inquired, whether he with the gods were come, or Suttung had destroyed him?

111. Odin, I believe, a ring-oath gave. Who in his faith will trust? Suttung defrauded, of his drink bereft, and Gunnlod made to weep!

112. Time 'tis to speak from the wise one's chair. By the well of Urd I silent sat, I saw and meditated, I listened to men's words.

113. Of runes I heard discourse, and of things divine, nor of graving them were they silent, nor of sage counsels, at the High One's hall. In the High One's hall. I thus heard say:

114. I counsel thee, Loddfafnir, to take advice: thou wilt profit if thou takest it. Rise not at night, unless to explore, or art compelled to go out.

115. I counsel thee, Loddfafnir, to take advice, thou wilt profit if thou takest it. In an enchantress's embrace thou mayest not sleep, so that in her arms she clasp thee.

116. She will be the cause that thou carest not for Thing or prince's words; food thou wilt shun and human joys; sorrowful wilt thou go to sleep.

117. I counsel thee, Loddfafnir, to take advice, thou wilt profit if thou takest it. Another's wife entice thou never to secret converse.

118. I counsel thee, Loddfafnir, to take advice, thou wilt profit if thou takest it. By fell or firth if thou have to travel, provide thee well with food.

119. I counsel thee, Loddfafnir, to take advice, thou wilt profit if thou takest it. A bad man let thou never know thy misfortunes; for from a bad man thou never wilt obtain a return for thy good will.

120. I saw mortally wound a man a wicked woman's words; a false tongue caused his death, and most unrighteously.

121. I counsel thee, Loddfafnir, to take advice, thou wilt profit if thou takest it. If thou knowest thou hast a friend, whom thou well canst trust, go oft to visit him; for with brushwood over-grown, and with high grass, is the way that no one treads.

122. I counsel thee, Loddfafnir, to take advice, thou wilt profit if thou takest it. A good man attract to thee in pleasant converse; and salutary speech learn while thou livest.

123. I counsel thee, Loddfafnir, to take advice, thou wilt profit if thou takest it. With thy friend be thou never first to quarrel. Care gnaws the heart, if thou to no one canst thy whole mind disclose.

124. I counsel thee, Loddfafnir, to take advice, thou wilt profit if thou takest it. Words thou never shouldst exchange with a witless fool;

125. For from an ill-conditioned man thou wilt never get a return for good; but a good man will bring thee favour by his praise.

126. There is a mingling of affection, where one can tell another all his mind. Everything is better than being with the deceitful. He is not another's friend who ever says as he says.

127. I counsel thee, Loddfafnir, to take advice, thou wilt profit if thou takest it. Even in three words quarrel not with a worse man: often the better yields, when the worse strikes.

128. I counsel thee, Loddfafnir, to take advice, thou wilt profit if thou takest it. Be not a shoemaker, nor a shaftmaker, unless for thyself it be; for a shoe if ill made, or a shaft if crooked, will call down evil on thee.

129. I counsel thee, Loddfafnir, to take advice, thou wilt profit if thou takest it. Wherever of injury thou knowest, regard that injury as thy own; and give to thy foes no peace.

130. I counsel thee, Loddfafnir, to take advice, thou wilt profit if thou takest it. Rejoiced at evil be thou never; but let good give thee pleasure.

131. I counsel thee, Loddfafnir, to take advice, thou wilt profit if thou takest it. In a battle look not up, (like swine the sons of men then become) that men may not fascinate thee.

132. If thou wilt induce a good woman to pleasant converse, thou must promise fair, and hold to it: no one turns from good if it can be got.

133. I enjoin thee to be wary, but not over wary; at drinking be thou most wary, and with another's wife; and thirdly, that thieves delude thee not.

134. With insult or derision treat thou never a guest or wayfarer. They often little know, who sit within, of what race they are who come.

135. Vices and virtues the sons of mortals bear in their breasts mingled; no one is so good that no failing attends him, nor so bad as to be good for nothing.

136. At a elder speaker laugh thou never; often is good that which the aged utter, oft from a shriveled hide discreet words issue; from those whose skin is sagging and decked with scars, and who go tottering among the vile.

137. I counsel thee, Loddfafnir, to take advice, thou wilt profit if thou takest it. Rail not at a guest, nor from thy gate thrust him; treat well the indigent; they will speak well of thee.

138. Strong is the bar that must be raised to admit all. Do thou give a penny, or they will call down on thee every ill in thy limbs.

139. I counsel thee, Loddfafnir, to take advice, thou wilt profit if thou takest it. Wherever thou beer drinkest, invoke to thee the power of earth; for earth is good against drink, fire for distempers, the oak for constipation, a corn-ear for sorcery, a hall for domestic strife. In bitter hates invoke the moon; the biter for bite-injuries is good; but runes against calamity; fluid let earth absorb.

ODIN'S RUNE POEM

ᚮᛑᛁᛋ ᚱᚨᛏᛘ ᚴᛜᛘᚨ

140. I know that I hung, on a wind-swept tree, nine whole nights, with a spear wounded, and to Odin offered, myself to myself; on that tree, of which no one knows from what root it springs.

141. Bread no one gave me, nor a horn of drink, downward I peered, to runes applied myself, wailing learnt them, then fell down thence.

142. Potent songs nine from the famed son I learned of Bolthorn, Bestla's sire, and a draught obtained of the precious mead, drawn from Odhrærir.

143. Then I began to bear fruit, and to know many things, to grow and well thrive: word by word I sought out words, fact by fact I sought out facts.

144. Runes thou wilt find, and explained characters, very large characters, very potent characters, which the great speaker depicted, and the high powers formed, and the powers' prince graved:

145. Odin among the Æsir, but among the Alfar, Dain, and Dvalin for the dwarfs, Asvid for the Jotuns: some I myself carved.

146. Knowest thou how to carve them? knowest thou how to expound them? knowest thou how to depict them? knowest thou how to prove them? knowest thou how to invoke? knowest thou how to sacrifice? knowest thou how to send? knowest thou how to consume?

147. 'Tis better not to pray than too much sacrifice; a gift ever looks to a return. 'Tis better not to send than too much consume. So Thund carved before the origin of men, where he ascended, to whence he afterwards came.

148. Those songs I know which the king's wife knows not nor son of man. Help the first is called, for that will help thee against strifes and cares.

149. For the second I know, what the sons of men require, who will as leeches live.

150. For the third I know, if I have great need to restrain my foes, the weapons' edge I deaden: of my adversaries nor arms nor wiles harm aught.

151. For the fourth I know, if men place bonds on my limbs, I so sing that I can walk; the fetter falls from my feet, and the manacle from my hands.

152. For the fifth I know, if I see a shot from a hostile hand, a shaft flying amid the host, so swift it cannot fly that I cannot halt it, if only I get sight of it.

153. For the sixth I know, if one wounds me with a green tree's roots; also if a man declares hatred to me, harm shall consume them sooner than me.

154. For the seventh I know, if a lofty house I see blaze o'er its inmates, so furiously it shall not burn that I cannot save it. That song I can sing.

155. For the eighth I know, what to all is useful to learn: where hatred grows among the sons of men—that I can quickly mediate.

156. For the ninth I know, if I stand in need my bark on the water to save, I can the wind on the waves allay, and the sea lull.

157. For the tenth I know, if I see troll-wives sporting in air, I can so operate that they will forsake their own forms, and their own minds.

158. For the eleventh I know, if I have to lead my ancient friends to battle, under their shields I sing, and with power they go safe to the fight, safe from the fight; safe on every side they go.

159. For the twelfth I know, if on a tree I see a corpse swinging from a halter, I can so carve and in runes depict, that the man shall walk, and with me converse.

160. For the thirteenth I know, if on a young man I sprinkle water, he shall not fall, though he into battle come: that man shall not sink before swords.

161. For the fourteenth I know, if in the society of men I have to name the gods, Æsir and Alfar, I know the distinctions of all. This few unskilled can do.

162. For the fifteenth I know what the dwarf Thiodreyrir sang before Delling's doors. Strength he sang to the Æsir, and to the Alfar prosperity, wisdom to Hroptatyr.

163. For the sixteenth I know, if a modest maiden's favour and affection I desire to possess, the soul I change of the white-armed damsel, and wholly turn her mind.

164. For the seventeenth I know, that that young maiden will reluctantly avoid me. These songs, Loddfafnir! thou wilt long have lacked; yet it may be good if thou understandest them, profitable if thou learnest them.

165. For the eighteenth I know that which I never teach to maid or wife of man, (all is better what one only knows. This is the closing of the songs) save her alone who clasps me in her arms, or is my sister.

166. Now are sung the High-one's songs, in the High-one's hall, to the sons of men all-useful, but useless to the Jotuns' sons. Hail to him who has sung them! Hail to him who knows them! May he profit who has learnt them! Hail to those who have listened to them!

TOTEMS

RUNES

TOTMS

The Icelandic Rune Poem

Wealth
>source of discord among kinsmen
>and fire of the sea
>and path of the serpent.

Shower
>lamentation of the clouds
>and ruin of the hay-harvest
>and abomination of the shepherd.

Giant
>torture of women
>and cliff-dweller
>and husband of a giantess.

God
>aged Gautr
>and prince of Ásgarðr
>and lord of Vallhalla.

Riding
> joy of the horsemen
> and speedy journey
> and toil of the steed.

Ulcer
> disease fatal to children
> and painful spot
> and abode of mortification.

Hail
> cold grain
> and shower of sleet
> and sickness of serpents.

Constraint
> grief of the bond-maid
> and state of oppression
> and toilsome work.

Ice
> bark of rivers
> and roof of the wave
> and destruction of the doomed.

Plenty
> boon to men

           and good summer
           and thriving crops.

Sun

           shield of the clouds
           and shining ray
           and destroyer of ice.

Týr

           god with one hand
           and leavings of the wolf
           and prince of temples.

Birch

           leafy twig
           and little tree
           and fresh young shrub.

Man

           delight of man
           and augmentation of the earth
           and adorner of ships.

Water

           eddying stream
           and broad geysir
           and land of the fish.

Yew

>	bent bow
>	and brittle iron
>	and giant of the arrow.

The Norwegian Rune Poem

1. Wealth is a source of discord among kinsmen;
   the wolf lives in the forest.

2. Dross comes from bad iron;
   the reindeer often races over the frozen snow.

3. Giant causes anguish to women;
   misfortune makes few men cheerful.

4. Estuary is the way of most journeys;
   but a scabbard is of swords.

5. Riding is said to be the worst thing for horses;
   Reginn forged the finest sword.

6. Ulcer is fatal to children;
   death makes a corpse pale.

7. Hail is the coldest of grain;
   Christ created the world of old.

8. Constraint gives scant choice;
   a naked man is chilled by the frost.

9. Ice we call the broad bridge;
   the blind man must be led.

10. Plenty is a boon to men;
    I say that Frothi was generous.

11. Sun is the light of the world;
    I bow to the divine decree.

12. Tyr is a one-handed god;
    often has the smith to blow.

13. Birch has the greenest leaves of any shrub;
    Loki was fortunate in his deceit.

14. Man is an augmentation of the dust;
    great is the claw of the hawk.

15. A waterfall is a River which falls from a mountain-side;
    but ornaments are of gold.

16. Yew is the greenest of trees in winter;
    it is wont to crackle when it burns.

The Anglo-Saxon

Rune Poem

Wealth is a comfort to all men;
> yet must every man bestow it freely,
> if he wish to gain honour in the sight of the Lord.

The aurochs is proud and has great horns;
> it is a very savage beast and fights with its horns;
> a great ranger of the moors, it is a creature of mettle.

The thorn is exceedingly sharp,
> an evil thing for any knight to touch,
> uncommonly severe on all who sit among them.

The mouth is the source of all language,
> a pillar of wisdom and a comfort to wise men,
> a blessing and a joy to every knight.

Riding seems easy to every warrior while he is indoors
> and very courageous to him who traverses the high-roads on the back of a stout horse.

The torch is known to every living man by its pale, bright flame;
> it always burns where princes sit within.

Generosity brings credit and honour, which support one's dignity;
> it furnishes help and subsistence
> to all broken men who are devoid of aught else.

Bliss he enjoys who knows not suffering, sorrow nor anxiety,
> and has prosperity and happiness and a good enough house.

Hail is the whitest of grain;
> it is whirled from the vault of heaven
> and is tossed about by gusts of wind
> and then it melts into water.

Trouble is oppressive to the heart;
> yet often it proves a source of help and salvation
> to the children of men, to everyone who heeds it betimes.

Ice is very cold and immeasurably slippery;
> it glistens as clear as glass and most like to gems;
> it is a floor wrought by the frost, fair to look upon.

Summer is a joy to men, when God, the holy King of Heaven,
>   suffers the earth to bring forth shining fruits
>   for rich and poor alike.

The yew is a tree with rough bark,
>   hard and fast in the earth,
>   supported by its roots,
>   a guardian of flame and a joy
>   upon an estate.

Peorth is a source of recreation and amusement to the great,
>   where warriors sit blithely together in the banqueting-hall.

The *Eolh*-sedge is mostly to be found in a marsh;

> it grows in the water and
> makes a ghastly wound,
> covering with blood every
> warrior who touches it.

The sun is ever a joy in the hopes of seafarers

> when they journey away over
> the fishes' bath,
> until the courser of the deep
> bears them to land.

Tiw is a guiding star; well does it keep faith with princes;

> it is ever on its course over the
> mists of night and never fails.

The poplar bears no fruit; yet without seed it brings forth suckers,
> for it is generated from its leaves.
> Splendid are its branches and gloriously adorned
> its lofty crown which reaches to the skies.

The horse is a joy to princes in the presence of warriors.
> A steed in the pride of its hoofs,
> when rich men on horseback bandy words about it;
> and it is ever a source of comfort to the restless.

The joyous man is dear to his kinsmen;
> yet every man is doomed to fail his fellow,
> since the Lord by his decree will commit the vile carrion to the earth.

The ocean seems interminable to men,
> if they venture on the rolling bark
> and the waves of the sea terrify them
> and the courser of the deep heed not its bridle.

Ing was first seen by men among the East-Danes,
> till, followed by his chariot,
> he departed eastwards over the waves.
> So the Heardingas named the hero.

An estate is very dear to every man,
> if he can enjoy there in his house
> whatever is right and proper in constant prosperity.

Day, the glorious light of the Creator, is sent by the Lord;
> it is beloved of men, a source of hope and happiness to rich and poor,
> and of service to all.

The oak fattens the flesh of pigs for the children of men.
> Often it traverses the gannet's bath,
> and the ocean proves whether the oak keeps faith
> in honourable fashion.

The ash is exceedingly high and precious to men.
> With its sturdy trunk it offers a stubborn resistance,
> though attacked by many a man.

Yr is a source of joy and honour to every prince and knight;
> it looks well on a horse and is a reliable equipment for a journey.

Iar is a river fish and yet it always feeds on land;
> it has a fair abode encompassed by water, where it lives in happiness.

The grave is horrible to every knight,
> when the corpse quickly begins to cool
> and is laid in the bosom of the dark earth.
> Prosperity declines, happiness passes away
> and covenants are broken.

TOTMS

TOTMS

TOTMS

Printed in Great Britain
by Amazon.co.uk, Ltd.,
Marston Gate.